Fact Finders®

CRACKING THE MEDIA LITERACY CODE

UNDERSTANDING THE NEWS

BY PAMELA DELL

CONSULTANT:
ROBERT L. MCCONNELL, PHD

CAPSTONE PRESS
a capstone imprint

Fact Finders Books are published by Capstone Press
1710 Roe Crest Drive, North Mankato, Minnesota 56003
www.mycapstone.com

Library of Congress Cataloging-in-Publication Data
Names: Dell, Pamela, author.
Title: Understanding the news / by Pamela Dell.
Description: North Mankato, Minnesota : Capstone Press, 2018. | Series: Fact
  finders: cracking the media literacy code
Identifiers: LCCN 2018016111 (print) | LCCN 2018019615 (ebook) | ISBN
  9781543527209 (eBook PDF) | ISBN 9781543527049 (library binding) | ISBN
  9781543527124 (paperback)
Subjects: LCSH: Media literacy—Juvenile literature. | Fake news—Juvenile
  literature.
Classification: LCC P96.M4 (ebook) | LCC P96.M4 D44 2018 (print) | DDC
  302.23—dc23
LC record available at https://lccn.loc.gov/2018016111

Editorial Credits
Michelle Bisson, editor; Russell Griesmer, designer; Jennifer Bergstrom, production artist; Morgan Walters,
media researcher; Tori Abraham, production specialist

Photo Credits
Alamy: North Wind Picture Archives, 11; Getty Images: Sion Touhig, 27; Library of Congress: Prints and
Photographs Division, 10; Newscom: Chandler NI Syndication, 9, Stillwell John/PA Photos/ABACA, 14,
Xinhua/Sipa USA, 21; Shutterstock: Alisara Zilch, design element throughout, balabolka, design element
throughout, Carolina K. Smith MD, 7, Christopher Penler, left 19, Eladora, (head) Cover, Kolonko, 4,
Macrovector, design element throughout, mikeledray, right 19, notkoo, (design element) Cover, Osugi, 13, Rob
Hainer, 17, rolandtopor, 29, roompoetliar, 24, sdecoret, 28, topform, design element throughout

Printed in the United States of America.
PA021

TABLE OF CONTENTS

CHAPTER 1

WHAT IS NEWS?

What's a common question people ask each other? How about "What's new?" It's not surprising, then, that what we call "the news" stems from that question. It's a fact that, century after century, people want to know what's going on in their world. That's what the news is all about.

Close to home, people are usually curious about what their friends, relatives, and neighbors are up to. News about movie stars, musicians, politicians, criminals, and sports figures are of interest to many. People are also interested in state, national, and world events. They want to know what is happening in science, the arts, and technology.

That's a lot of information to keep up with. So having the skills to sort through it is a big plus. It's a skill known as media literacy. Media literacy helps you tell the difference between fact and opinion and between trustworthy and questionable news. In these times of media overload, that skill has become essential.

 **What Is Media Literacy?**

The media are channels of mass communication. They include TV, radio, books, newspapers, the Internet, and much more. The term media literacy means developing thinking skills that help you judge what you see, hear, or read in the media. It's the ability to gather information from all media sources and **analyze** it in a fair and balanced way. Media literacy allows you to focus on what's true and important. You'll be better able to tell the difference between **unbiased**, fact-based news stories and fake ones.

 analyze—to make a detailed examination and explanation of something

unbiased—showing no strong favor either for or against something; being neutral

CHAPTER 2

THE MANY FORMS OF NEWS

News comes in many forms and from many sources. The most basic use of the word *news* refers to the reporting of events. A news story answers the questions, Who? What? When? Where? Why? and How? Good reporters try to be as objective and fact-based as possible. News stories do not include a reporter's personal point of view.

Sometimes a reporter's opinions or attitudes are made clear. Their articles are marked as commentary or opinion. These may include editorials, which express the opinions of a newspaper's editorial board. Reporters often write columns that focus on their areas of interest, usually from a particular point of view. Many newspapers also feature an op-ed page, which is short for opposite the editorial page. People outside the newspaper who have knowledge and a strong opinion on particular topics often write op-ed pieces.

objective—able to look at the facts without letting one's personal opinions or feelings get in the way

Most news outlets cover "what happened" the same way, but they differ in their analysis.

   As a result, a daily newspaper might have several pieces on the same news report. For example, the president signs a tax bill into law. The main story focuses on what happened. Another story analyzes what effects the law might have on people. An editorial expresses an opinion on whether the law is good or bad. An op-ed piece analyzes the law and its effects and gives an opinion. Many TV news shows also feature these various types of reporting. They just do them on the air rather than in print.

 commentary—spoken or written explanations or opinions about a particular subject

In earlier times information was passed along in ways that seem unusual now. But they made sense at the time.

Humans have used smoke signals, flashing lights, and drum beats to send important news. Carrier pigeons first delivered messages and news about 5,000 years ago. They continued to do so well into modern times. For a long time, travelers shared news at crossroads and around campfires. Messengers rode horses or ran from town to town delivering personal mail and official messages. Town criers shouted out the latest news and announcements to crowds gathered in towns and villages.

As time moved on, technology improved. A major breakthrough occurred in the mid-1400s. A German named Johannes Gutenberg invented a device that would change the world in a dramatic way. He invented the first practical printing press, which used metal, moveable type. This advancement meant that written works could be produced quickly. They were also cheaper and of better quality than before.

Billy was a World War II carrier pigeon. He was wounded on a mission, but recovered and went on to fly on many more missions.

Within 50 years of its invention, hundreds of thousands of books were in print throughout Europe. By 1500 there were 9 million books in print. By the early 1600s, as printing presses changed and evolved, the first newspapers began to appear. From there it was only a matter of time before cities around the world mass-produced newspapers on printing presses.

The Acta Diurna

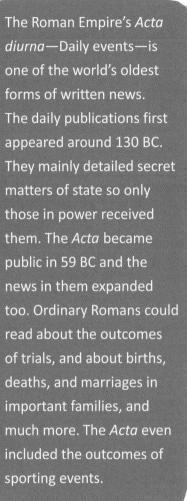

The Roman Empire's *Acta diurna*—Daily events—is one of the world's oldest forms of written news. The daily publications first appeared around 130 BC. They mainly detailed secret matters of state so only those in power received them. The *Acta* became public in 59 BC and the news in them expanded too. Ordinary Romans could read about the outcomes of trials, and about births, deaths, and marriages in important families, and much more. The *Acta* even included the outcomes of sporting events.

CHAPTER 3

FACT AND FICTION

The moon is occupied by mutant creatures that are half-human and half-bat!

Of course this is a ridiculous fiction. But in 1835 this sentence appeared in *The Sun*, a New York newspaper. *The Sun* offered readers stories like this to get them to buy the newspaper. And it worked.

The moon hoax got so popular that *The Sun* wrote a story about it in 1918.

Before *The Sun* appeared, U.S. newspapers generally focused on politics and world events. But *The Sun* and others like it were all about human-interest stories, mainly about crime and outrageous events. Sometimes the stories were entirely made up. *The Sun* was a roaring success, attracting thousands of readers. Its readers got their fill of "news" that stretched the truth. But many readers believed such news and bought the paper.

The Sun's circulation rose above 1 million readers in a short time.

The Sun started a trend. Other newspapers made lots of money printing stories that contained half-truths or lies presented as facts.

But some publishers fought back. Adolph Ochs, the publisher of *The New York Times*, and other publishers, tried to set the record straight. They fought lies with fact. The slogan of Ochs' paper, which he bought in 1896, was "All the news that's fit to print." That meant *The Times* only ran articles that met its standards of journalism. The articles had to be well-researched, fact-based, and objective. It was news people could trust. And it was not made up.

DID YOU KNOW?

Print news got competition from other media in the 20th century. Movies started to show newsreels in 1911. The first radio news broadcast took place in Detroit, Michigan, in 1920. Today that all-news station, WWJ, remains strong. TV began to take the place of newsreels in 1948, when the first regularly scheduled news shows aired in the United States.

The New York Times is trusted worldwide for its objective reporting of the news.

Plenty of other newspapers still follow those guidelines today. So do many radio and TV stations. But there are also modern versions of *The Sun* today in print, broadcasting, and on the Internet. Readers, viewers, and listeners have to pay close attention to decide what is true and what is made up.

★ journalism—the work of gathering and reporting news for newspapers, magazines, and TV

The Sun is still in business, and still sells made-up stories.

Today publishing isn't much different in some ways. There are newspapers with long, respected histories. They still do their best to provide accurate, factual news.

But newspapers with content like *The Sun*'s also still exist. The main difference may be that today both fact-based news and made-up stories are readily available elsewhere too. The Internet, including Facebook and many other popular sites, is a huge source of information. But that information isn't always reliable. It can range from totally true to factually false. It's important to look for the source of all the news you see online. Is it a newspaper or TV network you've heard of? If it isn't, think twice about believing it.

Social Media as a News Source

These days social media has a wide-ranging reach. Social media refers to the websites and apps that connect people through the Internet. Statistics from 2016 show that 4.2 billion users logged on to the top eight social media sites at least once a month. Those sites are Facebook, Twitter, Google+, YouTube, Instagram, Vine, Pinterest, and LinkedIn. Many of these users rely on social media to give them their daily news. But if you only get news from Facebook or Twitter, beware! Anyone can post anything and much of this so-called news is false and misleading.

Could we be tricked into believing that something crazy has happened when it's really made up news? We tend to think not, but in recent years plenty of false news has spread wildly. It has "gone viral" because people believed it to be true. Without checking the facts, many accept even crazy lies and pass them on. It is especially true when it's a "juicy" story or it supports something they already believe.

Part of the problem may be that serious news and entertainment news are often mixed together. For example, a clear separation once existed between TV news broadcasts and entertainment. Televised news was objective and fact-based reporting. Entertainment was for fun.

DID YOU KNOW?

From 1982 until 2016, public television aired the "The McLaughlin Group." Political commentators with different points of view discussed—and heatedly argued—the issues of the day. The program featured lively debates, which provided information and entertainment.

The CNN Center is full of windows so that it literally has "eyes on the world."

But then Cable News Network (CNN) came along in 1980 and changed everything. CNN aired 24 hours of nonstop news. Other cable networks were forced to compete by offering similar round-the-clock content. But that was a great deal of airtime to fill. It took a lot of resources. Plus, broadcasters needed content that would attract viewers. To do so they began creating a media mix of straight news, entertainment news, and, sometimes, strong opinion pieces.

The U.S. Federal Communications Commission (FCC) oversees the broadcasting industry. For much of the 20th century, it enforced the fairness doctrine. That policy required broadcasters to report on topics of public importance in a fair, honest, and balanced way. They were required to offer opposing views of any issue and not take sides. Because of the fairness doctrine, viewers saw and heard differing viewpoints on many issues.

The fairness doctrine ended in 1987. But parts of it remained until it was struck down entirely in 2011. Then it became the broadcasters' responsibility to air fair, honest, and balanced content. Once that happened, many broadcasters stopped spending the time and the money it took to produce shows with a balanced view.

People took sides on the fairness doctrine issue. Some were in favor of the change, arguing that the old rules had curbed free speech. Others said that without the rules viewers wouldn't be well informed on important topics. They wouldn't have enough information to make good decisions.

People have very strong views on immigration. Some are for it and some are against it. The fairness doctrine meant both views would be heard.

The shift in FCC rules has brought about another change. In many cases the news presenters and guests have become much more partisan. TV hosts and their guests often only give one side of a story. Viewers don't always check viewpoints other than those on the news shows they regularly watch. That means those viewers may have a biased or one-sided idea of the news.

★ partisan—strongly prejudiced in favor of one political group or cause

CHAPTER 4

21ST CENTURY CHALLENGE: RECOGNIZING THE REAL

Do young people know what is truthful news online? Stanford University researchers got shocking results when they investigated the question.

In 2015 and 2016 these researchers studied young people's "civic online reasoning." They wanted to find out how well young people do at judging information found online. The 7,804 responses came from students in middle school, high school, and college. The study focused on the flood of information that the students received on their smart phones, computers, and tablets.

The researchers found a surprising sameness in the students' skills. The results showed that the students had little ability to accurately judge online information. This, in turn, affected their ability to make smart judgments about that information.

Facebook founder Mark Zuckerberg was warned in fall 2016 that his site was home to a lot of false information. In September 2017 he publicly admitted that Facebook did have a major problem with false posts, false political advertisements, and other forms of bad information. In April 2018 Zuckerberg testified in front of Congress. He apologized for letting Facebook be used for fake news, election interference by foreign governments, hate speech, and invading people's privacy. "We didn't take a broad enough view of our responsibility, and that was a big mistake," Zuckerberg said, in a statement released to *The New York Times* and other newspapers the day before his appearance before Congress.

Zuckerberg vowed that the company would do better in the future. He also said the company had already taken steps to correct the abuses.

Mark Zuckerberg

Most students could not tell the difference between real and fake news. About 80 percent of the students thought sponsored advertisements were real news stories. They believed that fake Facebook and Instagram posts were real. Many students also accepted made-up comments on Twitter as real. Students often couldn't tell neutral, unbiased sites from sites with totally biased motives.

The researchers said that "Many assume that because young people are [good at using] social media they are equally [in the know] about what they find there. Our work shows the opposite."

The researchers concluded that much work needs to be done to increase students' media literacy.

DID YOU KNOW?

For more than 50 years, the Russian government has been actively spreading fake news—called disinformation—around the world. The fake news is meant to divide and cause fear in other countries.

Russia, Romania, and Macedonia are known to be the source of much of the fake news on the Internet. Many teenagers and young adults work in **troll** farms in these countries. They come up with false ads and stories. Then they post them online. The fake articles are often political and meant to influence public opinion and emotions.

Down on the (Troll) Farm

Russian troll farms purchased at least 3,000 Facebook ads during the 2016 U.S. presidential election season. The purpose of the ads was to influence how people voted. They were seen by as many as 10 million people. Some of the ads urged support for Donald Trump. Others focused on social issues or religion. Some were aimed at making Hillary Clinton, his opponent, look bad.

 sponsored advertisements—ads that sometimes look like regular articles or other content, but are paid for by advertisers in hopes people will be swayed to buy the product or service

 neutral—not taking sides in a conflict or disagreement

troll—a person who tries to start arguments on the Internet by posting false information or angry statements

Freedom of speech is at the heart of information found in newspapers, on the Internet, on TV, and on the radio. It is one of the most important rights promised in the First Amendment to the U.S. Constitution. It means that the government cannot stop people from

speaking or writing or publishing whatever they want. The one exception to that rule is speech that causes immediate harm.

DID YOU KNOW?

The *Oxford English Dictionary* chose "post-truth" as its word of the year in 2016. They chose it to reflect a world that finds truth less important than belief. Even more, a world in which public opinion is shaped more by appeals to emotion than to fact.

With few exceptions, people cannot be arrested for expressing their opinions. So, if it is nearly impossible to stop the publishing and posting of false information, what can we do? It is up to readers, viewers, and listeners to learn to tell the difference between real facts and fake. And there are proven ways to do this.

Would the Real Newspaper Please Stand Up?

Some people are experts at fooling the public. *The Denver Guardian* was recently called out by the real newspaper *The Denver Post*. *The Post* didn't want its reputation damaged by *The Guardian* and its **fraudulent** online articles that looked real. *The Denver Guardian* never had a hard copy edition as most papers do, but appeared only online. One of its false stories quoted the police chief of a nonexistent town. None of the stories it published could be found in other newspapers. The address listed for *The Guardian's* newsroom was a parking lot next to a vacant building. But the story and the **masthead** looked so real that many people believed it.

⭐ fraudulent—based on deceit

⭐ masthead—the name of a newspaper displayed at the top of the first page

CHAPTER 5

STAYING AHEAD OF THE GAME

Here are some helpful tips on how to tell the difference between good news websites and those that might be biased or even fake.

Look closely at the URL, the address at the top of a web browser. Some sites have names that intentionally include slight misspellings. If people don't notice, they end up being fooled. World-newss.com is an example. Note the added S on the word news. This is often a red alert. Rather than an innocent mistake, it's a sign that the site is fake. Also, pages that look sloppy or have a lot of errors in grammar, spelling, or punctuation are always suspicious.

Another red alert: Beware of URLs with strange or unusual extensions after the "dot." For instance, abcnews.com.co is fake. The real ABC news site is abcnews.go.com. The fake site has a .co at the end, a tricky change.

Two radio announcers started a rumor in 2001 that Britney Spears had died in a car crash. It quickly made headlines—and then was quickly corrected.

Always check a site's "About" page—if it has one. What you learn there should give clues about the site's accuracy. If there's no "About" page, you should also be suspicious.

If you read some "big news" on a site that's not a major news outlet, check the major news sites too. Trustworthy news sources will probably have the same story if it's true. If they don't, it might still be true. But investigate further to find out.

It takes good media literacy to look past the false claims and angry attitudes to find the facts. Telling the difference between fake news and real news takes the skills of an investigator. You follow the clues that lead to the truth. So when looking for trustworthy information, it's good to keep a few more pointers in mind.

For one, opinion and fact are two different things. A news story isn't fake just because you don't like what it says. Many politicians and others label facts they disagree with as "fake." The information may not be fake. It might just be that they don't like it.

Even the best and most trustworthy news organizations make mistakes. This is especially true when they're rushing to get the news out. A mistake is an accident. It is not intentionally fake news. A source you can trust will always try to quickly correct any mistakes they make.

And here's another thing to remember. Adults can be fooled just like kids can. So don't believe something is true because an adult said so. Find out for yourself.

Learn to tell the difference between real news, which is fact-based, and fake news, which is not. Media literacy—having a clear grasp of what's what—is the best way to learn how to tell truth from fiction.

HOW TO SPOT FAKE NEWS

FAKE NEWS

Consider the source
Click away from the story to investigate the site, its mission, and its contact info.

Read beyond
Headlines may be outrageous on purpose in an effort to get clicks. What's the whole story?

Check the author
Do a quick search on the author. Is s/he credible?

Check the date
Reposting old news stories doesn't mean they're relevant to current events.

Check your biases
Consider whether your own beliefs are affecting your judgment.

Supporting sources?
Click on those links. Determine if the info given actually supports the story.

Is it a joke?
If it is too outlandish, it might be satire. Research the site and author to be sure.

Ask the experts
Ask a librarian or consult a fact-checking site.

GLOSSARY

analyze (AN-uh-lize)—make a detailed examination and explanation of something

commentary (KOM-uhn-tare-ee)—spoken or written explanations or opinions about a particular subject

fraudulent (FRAWD-u-lent)—based on deceit

journalism (JUR-nuhl-iz-uhm)—the work of gathering and reporting news for newspapers, magazines, and TV

masthead (MAST-hed)—the name of a newspaper displayed at the top of the first page

neutral (NOO-truhl)—not taking sides in a conflict or disagreement

objective (uhb-JEK-tiv)—able to look at the facts without letting one's personal opinions or feelings get in the way

partisan (PAHR-tih-sahn)—strongly prejudiced in favor of one particular political group or cause

sponsored advertisements (SPON-surd ad-vuhr-TYZ-muhnts)—ads that sometimes look like regular articles or other content, but are paid for by advertisers in hopes people will be swayed to buy the product or service

troll (TROHL)—a person who tries to start arguments on the Internet by posting false information or angry statements

unbiased (uhn-BYE-uhst)—showing no strong favor either for or against something; being neutral

READ MORE

Hall, Homer L. *Student Journalism and Media Literacy.* New York: Rosen Publishing, 2015.

Hollingsworth, Tamara. *Unforgettable News Reports.* TIME for Kids Nonfiction Readers Series. Huntington Beach, Calif.: Teacher Created Materials, 2013.

Jennings, Brien. *Fact, Fiction, and Opinions: The Differences Between Ads, Blogs, News Reports, and Other Media.* North Mankato, Minn.: Capstone Press, 2018.

CRITICAL THINKING QUESTIONS

1. Who benefited from the elimination of the FCC's fairness doctrine and why? Do you think ending the fairness doctrine was a good or a bad idea? Explain your reasons.
2. How has the Internet helped the world keep up on current events? Has online news caused problems in recent years? If so, how and why?
3. What is the source of a great deal of fake news and fake advertising? Why might the posts be a danger to democracy? Do some research on your own to discover how those who create fake news can profit financially.

INTERNET SITES

Use FactHound to find Internet sites related to this book.

1. Visit *www.facthound.com*
2. Just type in 9781543527049 and go.

Super-cool stuff! Check out projects, games and lots more at
www.capstonekids.com

INDEX